HUGGING is my SUPERPOWER

Hugging is My Superpower

iUniverse books may be ordered through booksellers or by contacting:

iUniverse
1663 Liberty Drive
Bloomington, IN 47403
www.iuniverse.com
844-349-9409

ISBN: 978-1-6632-1959-6 (sc)
ISBN: 978-1-6632-1960-2 (e)

Print information available on the last page.

iUniverse rev. date: 03/09/2021

For my daughter Vivien
who I love to hug
and who loves to hug me

~ Dr. Danielle Hyles ~

HUGGING is my SUPERPOWER

story by: **Dr. Danielle Hyles**   illustrations by: **Enrico Iskandar**

Vivien loved to hug

In fact when she was born her two arms were up waiting for a hug from mommy or daddy

Vivien grew up and it was her first day at school

Vivien saw a boy and his name was Nico

She said, "hello"

And he signed his name

Vivien didn't understand so she gave him a hug

They were friends instantly

Vivien asked her teacher

"Why didn't he say hello to me?"

The teacher said,

"He did with his hands

It's called sign language"

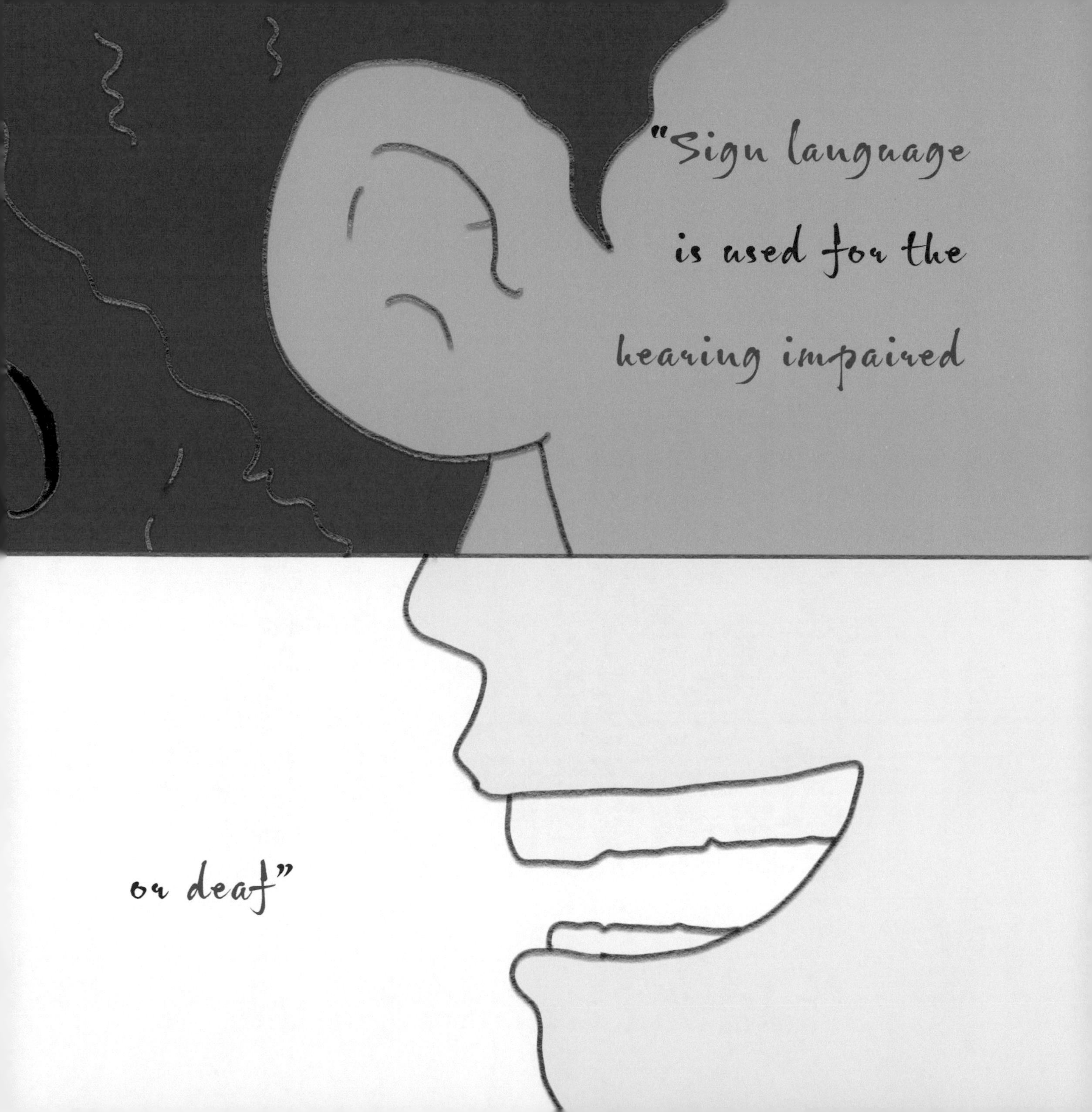
"Sign language
is used for the
hearing impaired
or deaf"

Vivien and Nico sat on the carpet

and did activities together

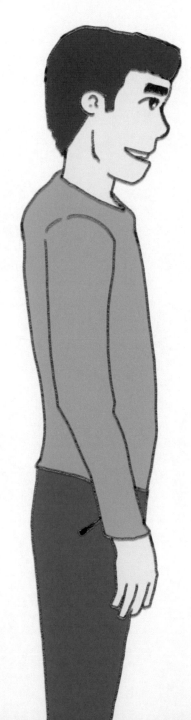

The teacher signed to Nico

"Why don't you teach

Vivien to sign"

Nico signed, "I'll start with the alphabet"

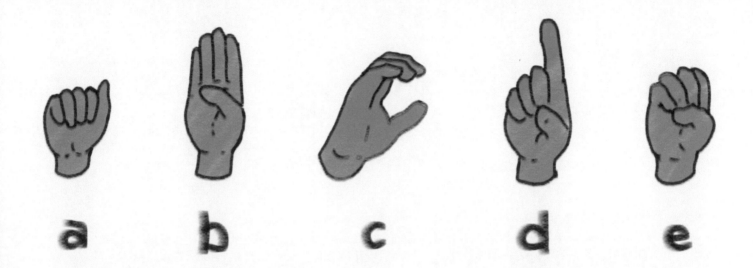

Nico began to teach Vivien the entire alphabet

Vivien is gifted and learns to sign quickly

v i v i e n

She says to Nico, "This is how you sign my name"

So Nico signed it back right away to Vivien

Vivien said, "that's right"

Then she signed his name

Nico said, "you got it"

Vivien loved to sing

But she got sad when she thought that her new friend

Nico couldn't hear her.

The teacher told Vivien to hold Nico's hands

and dance with him while she sings

Nico and Vivien had a good old time together

They became best friends

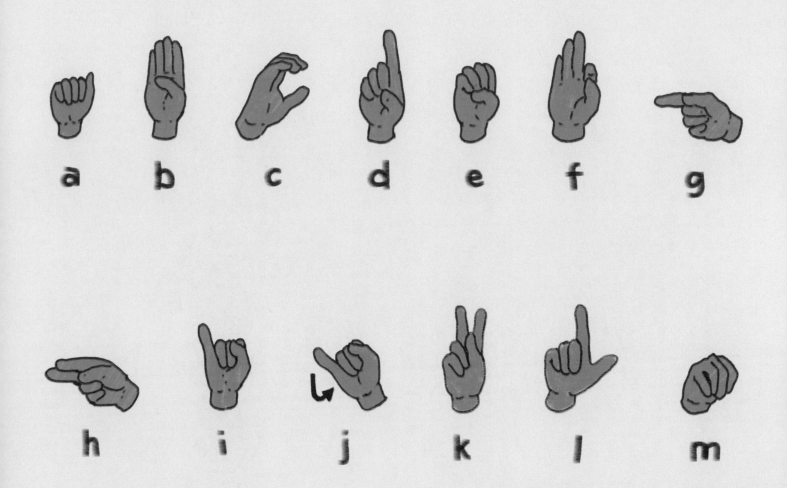

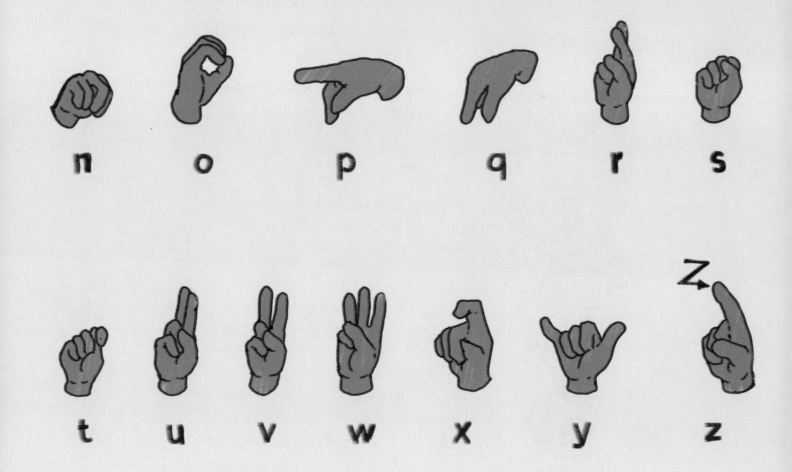

About the Author

Dr. Danielle Hyles is a Canadian author with Trinidadian heritage who is currently a school administrator with the Durham Catholic District School Board. She has written a research-based educational leadership book entitled "Bridging the Opportunity Gap" for educators all over the globe. She has also authored four children's books, "Loving My Working Mom", "Seeds of Belonging", "God's Children Are Math Wizards", and "We Can't Stop Now". "Hugging is My Superpower" is her fifth Children's book and explores communication through various forms.

Printed in the United States
by Baker & Taylor Publisher Services